Business Information Server, BIS

THE Killer App

World Greatest Crypto APP for development of Block-Chain + Real-Time Information Processing

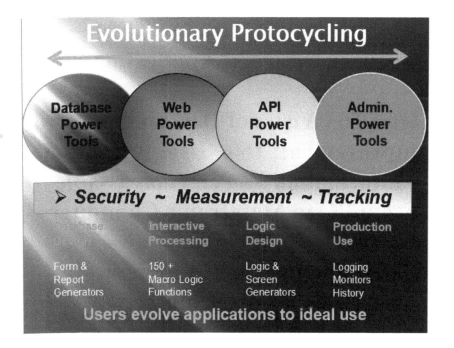

Business Information Server, BIS

THE Killer App

World Greatest Crypto APP:
Block-Chain + Real-Time
Information Processing

A REAL-TIME REPORT
PROCESSING SYSTEM
User Designed Applications

After 50+ Years of Development and Improvement; 150+ User Executable Information Power Tools Usable From PC to Mainframe Computers

The Unisys BIS System
By: Louis Schlueter

Real-Time Information Processing
The Unisys Business Information Server
BIS (aka MAPPER);
THE Killer App

BIS is the ideal, real-tme application development system for new, start up businesses or Crypto Application development. End users or professional developers can design reporting applications for each need that are upward compatible from a Windows Server PC to mid and mainframe system capabilities as operational growth develops. IT needs are perfectly matched to evolving business and Crypto World requirements with **user or professionaly designed applications**.

BIS is a powerful productivity APP for users on all systems.

These capabilities + its extremely fast database processing make BIS the ideal System for Block-Chain and Crypto information processing

Table of Contents

Business Information Server, BIS (MAPPER)
THE Killer App
World"Greatest Productivity APP.
Real-Time Report Processing

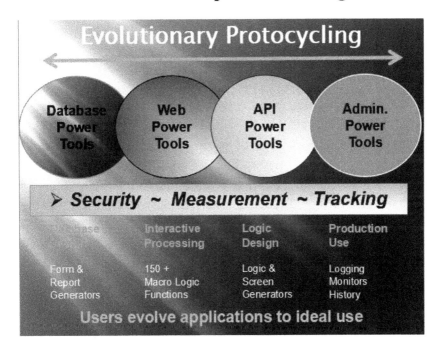

Preface

Real-Time Report Processing
The Unisys Business Information Server BIS (aka MAPPER);
The World's Greatest Productivity Killer APP
And Best Kept IT Secret

The story of its creation and evolution to "The World's Greatest Productivity APP and Real-Time Application Development Language for USERS is unique in the computer industry.

It offers enormous productivity potential by its unique, extensive functionality that supports Real-Time Information Processing and the ability of users to design their own data bases and applications without conventional programming.

This is a 1st, major Application Development Language for USERS. These capabilities + its extremely fast database processing make BIS the ideal System for Block-Chain and Crypto information processing

The BIS information processing system is more powerful and has greater general productivity potential than any software systems existing today. It has all the functionality and productivity producing potential of current software providing WORD PROCESSING, SPREAD SHEETS, GRAPHICS, EMAIL, INSTANT-MESSAGING, SEARCHING, MULT-LEVEL SORTING, EXTENSIVE CALCULATION, REAL-TME DATA BASE UPDATING

AND SHARING, FULL SECURITY USER AND DATA BASE MANAGEMENT AND INTERNET ACCESS. A full set of Coordination (Administrative) tools are available to manage and secure a dynamic, creative user Real-Time Information Processing environment.

All this capability is available today in one Business Information Server (BIS) system and available in hardware configurations providing upward application compatibility from PC's to Mid or Mainframe computers .

It is very likely you have never heard of this system and know nothing of its capabilities Though it was responsible for the sale of >$3 Billion of system sales in Manufacuring, Transportation, Distribution, Retailing, Banking, Insurance, Construction, Energy Production, Recreation, Federal State and City Governments and all the Military Branches.

The story of its creation and evolution to "The World's Greatest Productivity APP and Real-Time Application Development Language for USERS is unique in the computer industry.

It offers enormous productivity potential by its unique, extensive functionality that supports Real-Time Information Processing and the ability of users to design their own data bases and applications without conventional programming.

This is a 1st^h Application Development Language for USERS.

Since1968, Added analytic functional additions have been made almost every year since then, hence its functional richness, which is unequaled in the industry. BIS is the World's most powerful productivity APP. THE Killer APP.

User designed, Real-time Information Processing applications have enormous productivity potential and are applicable in the operation of all businesses and institutions from the smallest to the largest. Such productivity and upward compatibility across systems provide enormous tactical and competitive advantages for for BIS users.

There is a trend toward user-oriented computer systems, placing in the hands of the users the ability to direct computer power in application development. BIS is a giant step forward improving productivity with computer technology.

The Business Information Server, BIS Real-Time Information Processing systems, the subject of this book, make accessible to users powerful levels of productivity improvement that are impossible with conventional, structured, professional programming. The BIS system that provides Real-Time Information Processing capabilities, offers in <u>one integrated, hardware scalable software system, the World's Greatest, most powerful productivity APP</u>: THE Killer APP.

BIS Systems can operate across a wide range
of IndustryOpen systems
A user set of over 150 Information Power Tools
(Functions) with over 700 options interactively
executable without programming.
A true, real-time Report Structured Database with
interfaces to industry standard applications and data
bases.
A complete, Powerful End User Application
Development Language with Internet accessibility.
Client-Server Networking across a range of
system sizes and vendors.
A full set of system, user management and database
security controls.
Upward application expansion and compatibility from
MS Windows Server PC's to client-server and
individual or interconnected mainframe systems.

It is greater in productivity potential for all businesses and institutions than applications such as PC search engines, word processing and spread sheets combined.

These capabilities + its extremely fast database processing make BIS the ideal System for Block-Chain and Crypto information processing

Chapter 1

The Best Kept IT Secret System

The BIS information processing system is more powerful and has greater general productivity potential than any software systems existing today. It has all the analytic functionality and productivity producing potential of current software providing WORD PROCESSING, SPREAD SHEETS, GRAPHICS, EMAIL, INSTANT-MESSAGING, SEARCHING, MULT-LEVEL SORTING, EXTENSIVE CALCULATION, REAL-TME DATA BASE UPDATING, FULL SECURITY USER AND DATA BASE MANAGEMENT AND INTERNET ACCESS. A full set of Coordination (Administrative) tools are available to manage and secure a dynamic, creative user Real-Time Information Processing environment.

All this capability is available today in one Business Information Server (BIS) system and available in hardware configurations providing upward application compatibility from PC's to Mid or Mainframe computers .

It is very likely you have never heard of this system and know nothing of its capabilities. The story of its creation and evolution to "The World's Greatest Productivity APP is unique in the computer industry.

BIS offers the 1st Application Design Language for users. Its 50 year history precedes Microsoft PC-DOS and parallels that of its parent corporation named from Univac to Remington Rand Univac, to Sperry Univac, to Sperry to its current name of Unisys Corporation (the merger of Sperry and Burroughs Corporations). It sold over $3 Billion in systems for Sperry Corporation.

It offers enormous productivity potential by its unique, extensive functionality that supports Real-Time Information Processing and the ability of users to design their own data bases and applications without conventional programming.

Chapter 2

The Genesis of Real-Time Report Processing

The environment that led to the invention of the concepts and the creation of Real-Time Report Processing software was created in spite of and in opposition to the official policies of the parent corporation, Univac. The year was 1968. It all began in the Sperry Univac Manufacturing Plant in Roseville, Minnesota

In Feb. 1968, the author created a document entitled "418 Report Processing System" defining the concepts of general purpose Real-Time Report Processing and the system methods for implementing such capabilities. It described the 418 system hardware and software requirements:

Most importantly, the document described the concepts of general purpose Real-Time Report Processing which enabled users to establish reporting applications and process them **without having to program each application. The key was that the user's data became the command language to control Report Processing.**

EXAMPLE: Function command parameters in an Automobile Inventory Database:

```
     ENTER options:          AUTOMOBILE INVENTORY
 *    Make      . Model .  Number .   Price .                    .
 *Automobile .          . License .Wholsale. Retail   . Schedl . 1 .
 *-----------.-------.----------.--------.----------.--------.----
  ********** ******* ********* ******** ********* ******* ***
  BUICK   <Search for a single identity
  BUICK           CENTURY <[AND condition, search for 2 identities]
                          MLS5933 <[OR  search for 2 identities
                          MKL4371 < in same field]
                  5,000 <[Search in range, lower value
                R 15,000 <Search in range, upper value]
                  +         + <[Verticalsummation/subtotal]
          [Days difference between dates]> +        -
              Sort in alphabetic order]> 1
```

Etc. Full logical computational capabilities are possible. Any number of fields or combinations of Parameters and options can be used.

The point is that data and intuitively obvious command parameters are submitted in the context of the user's own data. Reports can be formed as above or they can contain textual or graphic information or any combination of these.

This is why users find Real-Time Report Processing so easy to understand and use. Their own data becomes the command language for Report Processing.

The initial Report Processing System was first done on the 418 Univac Computer system and was expanded to the 1100 Mainframe systems and named the MAPPER System.

During the design of the initial MAPPER 1100 system software, the existing functionality of 418 CRT-RPS was duplicated. This consisted of the following:

User Sign-on and off,
Mode (File Cabinet) Switching,
Form Generation (New Type of Reporting)
Report Index, Add, Delete, Duplicate, Display,
Line Roll, Add, Delete and Duplicate,
Search Single or Multiple Reports for single ID's,
Sort Reports or Results,
Find and Display (positional search),
Match data between reports,
Arithmetic and Totalize data analysis,
System High Speed and Remote Printing
Punch Card output,
Report Build Generation, RBG
Report Generation, RPG

New analytic functionality was added; multi-id search, fast access function call techniques, password security for data access, and RPG (Report Generation) with Match capability and Station to Station (Email like) messaging.

The First MAPPER 1100 operations began in February of 1975 on an 1106 main-frame system.

By the end of 1975 over 250 terminals were configured for access to the IS&C MAPPER 1100 system. Most of the departments in the Roseville plant had user developed, operational, Real-Time Report Processing applications:

Production Control	Final Assembly,
Scheduling and Dispatching,	Shipping,
Quality and Reliability Control,	Site administration,
Final Test,	Transportation,
Purchasing,	DevelopmentCenter
Material Support,	Engineering, Drafting, etc.
Cost Accounting,	IS&C Project Status
Receiving,	

In addition to the Roseville plants, services were also provided to Sperry factory operations in:

Eagan MN,	Bristol TN,
Jackson MN,	Chicago IL,
MontrealCanada,	Elk Grove IL,
Utica NY,	Philadelphia PA,
Salt Lake City UT,	Cupertino CA.

Administrative reporting was also provided to departments in Univac Headquarters, Blue Bell PA.. Over 375 different types (applications) of reporting consisting of 1,500,000 lines of report data was available on line for real-time Report Processing.

Marketing offices did administrative reporting from:

Minneapolis MN,	Phoenix AZ,
Blue Bell PA,	Washington DC,
Whitpain PA,	Indianapolis IN,
Toronto Canada,	Atlanta GA,
Des Moines IA,	San Francisco CA,
New York NY,	Chicago IL,
Dallas TX,	Houston TX,
Montclair NJ,	San Antonio TX,
Cleveland OH,	Tulsa OK, etc.
Kansas City MO,	

Chapter 3

This use of Real-Time Report Processing services by marketing for administrative purposes provided marketing exposure to these concepts which was instrumental in the development of the MAPPER 1100 market in the future.

MAPPER 1100 Transition to Marketing

MAPPER 1100

CRT Report Processing System

UNISCOPE
Visual Communication Terminal

MAPPER 1100 was not to be offered to Univac customers. It was only to be used internally in the corporation. How ever, A Chicago salesman made the first sale of MAPPER 1100 to Santa Fe Railway in 1976.

Santa Fe Railway, The First MAPPER 1100 Customer

The story of the use of MAPPER 1100 at Santa Fe Railway is truly remarkable and a great example of the potentials of user-designed applications as done with Real-Time Report Processing systems.

By 1982, over 2,500 terminals were on-line tracking over 68,000 cars in over 175 rail yards. The system used two Sperry 1100/84 central multi-processors and had a total value of over $25 Million.

 By 1978 other 1100 main frame computer system sales based on MAPPER 1100 were also made to GTE Automatic Electric, FTD Florists and Sargent Lundy Engineering corporations, the Chicago Board of Education, Kansas City Power and Light.

Chapter 4

System Evolution

More improvements and functionality were added. The view of the on-line report database was redefined to be more understandable by users. It was compared to a room full of "Electronic Filing Cabinets" easily understood by users.

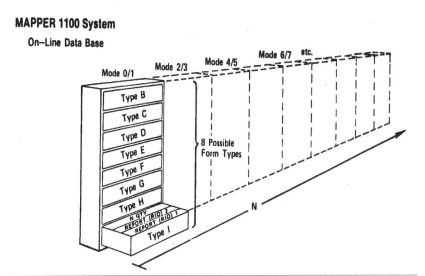

MAPPER 1100 System
On–Line Data Base

A large set of real-time, manually executed update, selection and computational analytic functions were provided:

A	Fortran-based equation calculator
ADON	Append a function Result or report to another report
AL	Alarm message reminder on a specified time and date.
AR	Add a report
AUX	Print reports on auxiliary printers
BATCHSTRT	Batch Processing start function
BATCHPORT	Batch processing port input
BF	Binary find process (Search and display to a data position)

CHG	Locate and change (update) a character string
COPY	Copy files from system to system
D	Display a report
DATE	Analyze dates within a report
DR	Delete a report
ELT	Copy a report to program file
F	Find characters in a report/reports
FORM	Form design and generation
I	Index a form Type (Drawer)
LINE-ADD,DEL	Line add, delete,
DUP,INS	Line duplicate, insert
LOC	Locate character string and display at that point in the report
MA	Match data in two reports
MAU	Match two reports and update
PR	Print a report or reports or result
PSW	Report update password
REP	Replace report with result/report
RET	Retrieve a file or element from other database outside of the RPS
RETR	Retrieve a report from history
RF	Reformat an existing report
RPSW	Report read access password
S	Search a report or reports in a type
SEND	Terminal to terminal report transmit
SORT	Sort a report or result
SS	Station to station message transfer
SU	Search report/s and update changes
TOT	Perform arithmetic on report data

MAPPER Real-Time Report Processing provides access from a distributed network of terminals to a commonly accessible report database. These reports could be displayed and updated within security limitations and, once updated; the changes could be seen immediately by anyone displaying the report, no SAVE required by users.

While real-time report data visibility and updating is extremely valuable, it is the processing of the reports using the manual functions to create Real Control Information where enormous productivity gains can be made.

These analytic functions process individual lines or reports or sets of reports within a Type of reports. When executed, these analytic functions produce full data sets called **Results**. This is different than a result produced by most PC information processors which usually only produce a screen of processed data at a time.

These Results could be further processed or refined using other functions. It is possible to process either Reports or Results with these functions. This is one of the characteristics that distinguishes MAPPER Real-Time Report Processing from typical PC information processing people see today.

Where repetitive patterns are encountered in the use of manual functions, RUN scripted procedures could be created that could execute the same function sequence with a single call.

EXAMPLE REPORT

```
.DATE    09 DEC 20  04:30:11  RID    2B   30 OCT 20  MAPCOORD
.Production Status Report          Corporate Production       B0002
*St.Status.By.Product   .Serial.Produc.Order.Cust.Produc.Produc.Ship
*CD. Date .IN. Type     .Number. Cost .Numbr.Code. Plan .Actual.Date
*==.======.==.==========.======.======.=====.====.======.======.====
 IP 201224 LS BLACKBOX1 436767        20389 AMCO 201223 201224
 IP 201225 LS BLACKBOX1 436768        20390 AMCO 201223 201225
 IP 201219 LS BLACKBOX2 637071        20353 INTR 201218 201219
 OR 200110 LS BLACKBOX4               94754 ARCO
 SC 200110 LS BLACKBOX5 675281        97441 FEDS 200131
                                  .
                                  .
                                  .
 IP 201222 LS BLACKBOX5 737582        20040 AMCO 201222 201222
 SH 201222 LS BLACKBOX0 746327        54327 FEDS 201201 201202
 SH 201222 LS BLACKBOX6 368061        54438 FEDS 201201 201202
 SH 201209 LS BLACKBOX6 777324        54232 DICO 201207 201209
 SH 201203 LS BLACKBOX6 785367        52232 INTR 201207 201203
 IP 201216 LS BLACKBOX6 926581        89381 INTR 201215 201216
                    ***** END REPORT *****
```

SEARCH REQUEST

When a request is made to process a report or set of reports, a Function Mask is displayed which consists of the headers from the report/s to be processed.

Parameter data is entered in the field/s to be processed below the headers. The Functions have options which can be entered in the line above the mask. The line Of *'s below the headers are used to control the processing of individual Character positions within the fields. The presence of an * means that character position will be processed. This is a search for shipped (SH) status.

```
                    SEARCH REQUEST FUNCTION MASK
*St.Status.By. Product .Serial.Produc.Order.Cust.Produc.Produc.
*Cd. Date .In.  Type    .Number. Cost .Numbr.Code. Plan .Actual. Date .Order.Cod.
*==.======.==.=========.======.======.=====.====.======.======.======.====
 ** ****** ** ********* ****** ****** ********** ****** ****** ****** ***** ***
 SH
SEARCH RESULT PRODUCED. Compare this to a typical non specific Google Search Result.


                    .                      .  . .
                .  8 LINES FOUND, 42 SEARCHED
                            SH

                .DATE   04 SEP 20  10:17:30  RID    2B   30 OCT 20  MICRO
 .Production Status Report                    Corporate Production          B0002
 *St.Status.By. Product .Serial.Produc.Order.Cust.Produc.Produc. Ship .Ship .Spc.
 *Cd. Date .In.  Type    .Number. Cost .Numbr.Code. Plan .Actual. Cod.
 *==.======.==.=========.======.======.=====.====.======.======.======.
  SH 201203 LS BLACKBOX0 746327        54237 FEDS 201201 201202 201203 S8738
  SH 201202 LS BLACKBOX6 368061        54438 FEDS 201201 201201 201202 S6937
  SH 201209 LS BLACKBOX6 777324        54232 DICO 201207 201208 201209 S8538
  SH 201203 LS BLACKBOX6 785367        52203 ARCO 201201 201202 201203 S8934
  SH 201202 LS BLACKBOX7 744627        44232 INTR 201201 201201 201202 S8531
  SH 201203 LS BLACKBOX8 945327        74272 FEDS 201201 201202 201203 S8518
  SH 201204 LS BLACKBOX9 714577        64231 AMCO 201201 201203 201204 S8531
  SH 201206 LS GREENBOX7 669624        54682 AMCO 201201 201205 201206 S8553
                    ***** END REPORT *****
```

A key to the "user friendly" simplicity of the MAPPER
language is the fact that intuitively obvious function
parameters are submitted in the context of the user's
own data. When they design the data form, they automatically
create an application specific function control language.

```
        EXAMPLES OF SEARCH INPUT PARAMETERS AND OPTIONS

              H (Option,Delete search statistics)
*St.Status.By. Product .Serial.Produc.Order.Cust.Produc.Produc. Ship .Ship .Spc.
*Cd. Date .In.  Type    .Number. Cost .Numbr.Code. Plan .Actual. Date .Order.Cod.
*==.======.==.=========.======.======.=====.====.======.======.======.=====.===.
 ** ****** ** ********* ****** ****** ***** **** ****** ****** ****** ***** ***
 SH                       Single identifier

 SC                       Multiple
 SH                       identifiers

 SH           BLACKBOX/    AND condition with last character masked

              500000      Search in
 R            700000      Range
```

Any number of fields can be searched at the same time. Consider these extensive Search
Options as compared to a limited Google search for key words.

EXAMPLES OF SORT INPUT PARAMETERS

```
*St.Status.By.  Produ  .Serial.Produc.Order.Cust.Produc.Produc.Spc.
*Cd. Date .In.  Type   .Number. Cost .Numbr.Code. Plan .Actual.Cod.
*==.======.==.=========.======.======.=====.====.======.======.====
** ****** ** ********* ****** ****** ***** **** ****** ****** ****
   1                        Single level sort, ascending order

   1D                       Single level sort, descending order

   1          2   Multiple level sort, both ascending

   1          2D  Multi-level, next ascending, 2nd descending
```

EXAMPLES OF TOTALIZER INPUT PARAMETERS

```
*Product  . Sub .Produc. Whole . Retail .Commiss.Space.
*Type     . Key .Cost  . Cost  . Sale$  .Charge .Req  .Quantity.
*=========.=====.======.=======.========.=======.=====.========.===
********* ***** ****** ******* ******** ******* ***** ******** **
Multiple vertical sums  +       +        +        +

Algebraic sums  +       -       +        -                 =

Horizontal multiply             *        =                 +
and vertical sum                         +

Adjust all       +10
                             Costs +10        =

Subtotals  S     +        + when Key changes

Averages         A     A     A        A

Subtotal   S     +              and Grand Cumulate   C
```

Besides the users having the ability to selectively and manually execute Real-Time Report Processing functions, the RUN scripted language continued to develop into a powerful scripted application design language. The users could learn this RUN script language and build powerful applications. One of the reasons this language could be readily understood by users is the fact that much of it is derived directly from the steps of manual function execution.

For example, to execute a manual Search function, the report/s to be processed would be specified: (This would search all the reports in the B Drawer.)

SEARCH REPORT
Report or Drawer B_____
Format Number _____

The Function Mask would then be displayed:

```
*St.Status.By. Product .Serial.Produc.Order.Cust.Produc.Produc. Ship .Ship .Spc.
*Cd. Date .In.  Type   .Number. Cost .Numbr.Code. Plan .Actual. Date .Order.Cod.
*==.======.==.=========.======.======.=====.====.======.======.======.====.===.
** ****** ** ********* ****** ****** ***** **** ****** ****** ****** **** ***
SH
```

The equivalent RUN language script statement format for this process would be:

```
@SRH,B H 'STCD' *,SH .
                |____ Data to be searched for.
           |_____ Field to be searched.
       |_____ H option
   |_____ All reports in B Drawer to be searched.
 |_____ Search command.
```

All the 150+ executable Real-Time Report Processing functions have equivalent RUN script statements. Thus, they all become powerful script statements in the RUN script language. When the users become experienced in using the manual functions and how they can be used in Real-Time Report Processing, they can be excellent RUN script designers because they know exactly how to use these analytic functions and what they can do.

In RUN script design, in addition to all the manual functions being usable, a full repertoire of RUN script statements for variable specification and control are also available as well full evaluation (IF,THEN) logic control. The ability to read and update individual lines of data with RUN control could be done. In the early stages, basic screen text formation and output could be done as well as screen input with variable data. In time, the RUN script language would become a truly complete, structured, application script language capable of the most modern designs and appearance.

The Efficient Report Structured Database

Usage studies showed that the average report consisted of 500 lines (record sets) or less of data. This was a natural data sizing characteristic for this Real-Time Report Processing service. Also, it was noted that, because most of the report data consisted of lines containing a consistent number of fields of data, most lines for a given application were the same length and consumed the same amount of space in storage.

Based on these facts, pertinent to the unique nature of this service, report formatting was organized in a new data concept as a set of contiguous relative data in storage. This contiguous report data set made it possible to eliminate record linkage as well as record scattering. It also made it possible to eliminate the line tables and associated line table maintenance. These changes dramatically improved the efficiency of database performance in this real-time, random access and Real-Time Report Processing service environment.

These concepts, when implemented, completed the evolution to the Report Structured Database concepts that constitute the modern database concepts used in the current Unisys BIS, Business Information Server Real-Time Report Processing systems. They are capable of supporting very large volumes of random-access reporting simultaneously accessed from many terminals as well as high volumes of real-time updating.

This Report Structured Database concept is ideal to support the random processing and updating associated with the computerization of real time, real-control information processing. Performance also remains consistent throughout the operating day with no record scattering deterioration. It is also a database concept that is simple enough for users to understand, organize and manage their report data. In later versions of the systems, it also is possible to organize the base with indexing and algorithmic structures for larger quantities of data.

Chapter 5

The Unisys MAPPER 1100 System Service Expansion

From the examples of Real-Time Report Processing done by the initial Test and Production Control departments, other users could see the benefits of Real-Time Report Processing. Most departments were frustrated with their ability to get their specialized information processing needs satisfied by conventional programming provided by the IS&C department.

So when they saw that they could develop their own applications with MAPPER Real-Time Report Processing their enthusiasm was immediate. After hour MAPPER Real-Time Report Processing training classes were set up by the Education department to educate new potential users.

The IS&C Western Utility Computing Center provided the primary MAPPER 1100 Report Processing services to Sperry Univac plants. By 1978 this MAPPER service had grown to a major information processing asset provided by IS&C Through out the corporation.

Main Frame Central Processor – U1100/81 with Magnetic Tape, Disc and Drum storage and 2 High Speed Printers.

Over 480 Uniscope display terminals connected.

Factories & Departments Serviced:

Roseville, Plant 4, Building 1.

Mfg Production Control
Units and Systems Final Test
Industrial and Production Engineering
Factory Scheduling and Planning
Factory Quality
Preproduction Manufacturing
Purchasing

Site Administration
Diagnostic Programming
Factory Operations
Plant Engineering and Maintenance
Central MAPPER Coordination
Information Systems & Control (IS&C)

Roseville, Plant 2, Building 2.

Manufacturing Production Control
Midwest Region Computer Center
Support Engineering (field changes)
Technical Field Support
Material Support Liaison
Tear Down and Shipping

Roseville, Plant 3, Building 3.

Product Engineering
Project Planning and Reporting
Software Development and Support
General Services
Personnel
Marketing
Engineering Information Service Center
Publications and Specifications
Systems Support

Roseville, Plant 4, Building 4.

Manufacturing Production Control
Factory Quality
Receiving Stores and Crib
Finished Goods Inventory
Traffic and Shipping
Purchased Material Quality
Worldwide Semiconductor Facility
Returned Rental Equipment

Satellite Plants

Montreal Canada - Power Supply Manufacturing
Salt Lake City, Utah - Printed Circuit Facility
Jackson, Minnesota - Printed Circuit Manufacturing
Clear Lake, Iowa - Test and General Manufacturing

Dial-In Service, National

Corporate Administration, Philadelphia
Marketing Support, Philadelphia
Marketing Branches
Marketing Central Operations, Chicago
Product Development Liaison, Philadelphia
Customer Engineering, Philadelphia
Worldwide Marketing Development
Sperry Internal Auditing
IS&C Headquarters, Philadelphia
Asset Management, Philadelphia

MAPPER 1100 Real-Time Report Processing
Transactional Daily Activity

Over 170,000 total transactions
Over 40,000,000 lines of data processed
Over 20,000 updates (equivalent to 100,000
punched cards)
Over 10,000 searches of report/s
Over 30,000 Totalizations, Sorts,
RUN Script executions
Over 7,000 printouts and messages

MAPPER 1100 Real-Time Report Processing Database

Over 2,500,000 lines of report data on-line
Over 675 different kinds of **user designed** reporting applications
Over 10,000 individual reports

Extensive historical reports available

Other MRCC System Real-Time and Batch Processing

Real-time Transaction Processing System (TPS)
This is COBOL-DMS based. Over 40,000
transactions are done in this system along with
the MAPPER service.

MAPPER 1100 Batch Interface
With MAPPER Batch Start and Retrieve functions,
users can start batch RUNs with MAPPER data included.
They can also retrieve files from the batch
environment   into the MAPPER database.

**This MAPPER service with over 675 <u>user-designed</u>
applications was a major profitable asset to the users, IS&C
and the Corporation. Marketing used it as a show case to
illustrate the reality and possibilities of Real-Time Report
Processing by bringing prospective customers in for plant
tours or to see demonstrations done in the marketing branches.
This accelerated the pressure to make MAPPER 1100 a
corporate supported and marketed product.**

Chapter 6

MAPPER 1100 System– Coordination and Control

As the service grew, it became obvious that it was necessary to manage system resources by monitoring database growth and Real-Time Report Processing function use. **Users are restricted to which Real-Time Report Processing functions and RUNs they can use. Security control could be effectively tailored to each individual user's and application needs.**

The Coordinator (Administrator) is provided tools that ensure secure individual use and database efficiencies are available. **The ability to create a user safe, creative design environment was key to implementing user-designed computing and gain the full productivity benefits possible.**

Tools for function execution management are available. An internal logging process is created which records these characteristics for each transaction chronologically into a Transaction Log:

User department
User name
Function start date
Function start time
Function end time
Name of function executed
Number of executing terminal
Function duration time
Report/s data lines processed
Number of I/O's, storage access
Number of breakpoints (function interrupts)

A Log List Function is provided which provides the means to analyze function activity by any criteria. We ca examine any time period. We can look at activity at certain stations or by certain users or whole departments.. We can look at high-impact functions by looking at the number of I/Os or breakpoint frequencies. We can examine specific functions in

detail and thereby pinpoint how to improve efficiencies to gain ideal results.

One of the most exciting aspects of watching proper, user-oriented, Real-Time Report Processing implementation in a user-community is to see the multifaceted ingenuity and innovative adaptation of computing power in the Real-Time Report Processing environment.

Ideal Coordination would create a Real-Time Report Processing environment where the users had an illusion of infinite capability.

Chapter 7

MAPPER System Development & Evolution

This Chapter describes marketing expansion and full functional MAPPER development. The characteristics of large-scale, real-time, user application design and implementation is also described.

By 1980 MAPPER 1100 sales had been made to Santa Fe Railroad, FTD Florists, Sargent Lundy Engineering and Kansas City Power and Light corporations and the Chicago Board of Education.

The reputation of MAPPER 1100 had also been recognized by international marketing, In 1981 it was authorized as a Category I, fully supported product available throughout the world.

The success of MAPPER with 1100 systems made it an obvious choice to be offered for use with UNIX systems. This was called U Series MAPPER or MAPPER C software.

MAPPER software is unique in the industry in this ability to do application migration across PC to Mainfraim systems without application conversion. In 1992, UNIX MAPPER Software was the first XOPEN application listed in the

XOPEN

X/Open Compliancy

- X/Open Registered Application
- Achieved certification on March 6, 1992
- Enrolled as the "first application" in the X/Open Application Registration directory

registry.

Eventually over 500 Main Frame MAPPER 1100 systems were sold in *Japan.*

In 1985, a Chinese micro-MAPPER system was also created. With Sperry's help, a factory was set up in China to manufacture the Chinese micro-MAPPER systems. It had an enormous keyboard which represented a repertoire of Chinese language characters. This version of MAPPER Real-Time Report Processing had a limited success but it did indicate the universal appeal of this kind of information processing.

```
.DATE 01 APR 85  14:21:04  RID      14    26 MAR 85  HANS
               SYSTEM MESSAGES                                      G0074
*====================================================================
```

PRESENTED TO

MR. H.A. TYABJI

这是第一个中文 MAPPER 系统的示范

ON THE OCCASION
OF THE FIRST DEMONSTRATION
OF CHINESE LANGUAGE MAPPER

一九八五年三月二十八日

28 MARCH 1985

N.A. BLACK

H.F. LIU
刘洪发

S. WONG

J. ELBNER

W.N. LIU
刘卫民

Z.Z. XU
徐志忠

H. HERMANS

W. MEINEL

J-P. ZUNDEL

As the MAPPER market grew in the US and internationally, the users proved their creativity by providing a steady stream of analytic functional feature enhancement suggestions. New, major analytic functional releases were made almost annually. By the end of the Sperry Corporate era, a powerful array of Real-Time Report Processing functions, Information Power Tools, were created that is unique in the IT industry today.

MAPPER Real-Time Report Processing Information Power Tools; 150 analytic functions with 700+ options

Abort Process
Acknowledge Message
Add Line/s
Add On Report/Result
Add Report
Alpha to Octal Data Converter
Append Data Line/s
Arithmetic (Formula Solution)
Auxiliary Printers
Add new Report
Alpha to Octal Data Converter
Append Data Lines
Arithmetic Algebraic Formula
Solution
Background RUN
Batch Process Interface
Binary Find
Cabinet Switch
Calculate (Line By Line Logic)
Calculate & Update Data
Calendar Generation
Change Character String
Display Colors Control
Horizontal Character Count
Combine Report Data
Communications Output
Printer
Compare Report Data

Count Statistical Analysis
Create File In 1100
Create Help Result Extract
Create Temporary Result Copy
Create Temporary Data Format
Date & Time Computation
Decode Encoded Report
Delete Selected Data
Delete Line/s
Delete Report
Device Definition
Device Mapping
Display Format
Display Graphics
Display Report
Display/Hold Headings
DLC (Display Line Numbers)
Drawer List (DL)
Drawer Password
Drawer Table of Contents
Duplicate Line/s
Duplicate Report
Encode Report
Extract Data
Field Column Count
Find & Diplay At Location
Form Generation
Form Design

On-line User Help	Password Entry
Hold Characters On Screen	Print To System Printer
Hold Lines On Screen	Reform Form
Index Drawer	Reformat Report
Index User	Release Display
Insert Line/s	Remote System RUNs
Iterative Binary Find	Replace Report
Iterative Calculate	Report & Line Limits Display
Iterative Count	Report List
Iterative Date Analysis	Resume Process
Iterative Find	Retrieve System File
Iterative RUNs	Report Writer
Iterative Search	Save Report Version
Iterative Sort	Search Report/s
Iterative Totalize	Search Update Report/s
Language Switch	Send Report Station To Station
Line Control	(E-mail)
Line Data Statistics	Send Report to User (E-mail)
List Dictionary Data	On-line Coordinator Help
Locate & Display Character	Horizontal Shift Display
String	Sign Off
Locate Help Keywords	Sign On
Match Report Data	Sort Report
Match & Update Report Data	Sort & Replace Report
Move Data Line/s	Start System Program
Name Report	System Activity Display
Names List	Totalize Report Data
Octal to Alpha Data	Undo Previous Data Change
Conversion	UNIX Linux OS Interface
Repaint Screen	Update From Search/Match

These real-time Report Processing functions can be used by any user without programming. Each function can be turned on or off for each user if needed for security control. The users are limited only by their imagination, creative ability and system security policies. **An illusion of infinite capability can be created for users.**

With the availability of graphic and color display terminals and
PCs graphic chart functions were created. These could create:

Bar Charts	Radar Charts
Block Charts	Scatter Charts
Line Charts	Target Charts
Mixed Bar and Text Charts	
Line Charts	Pareto Charts
3D Bar Charts	Time Line Charts
RADAR Chart	Scatter Chart
Multiple Chart	Organization Chart
Sign Maker	Graphics Scaler
Target Chart	Text Chart
Time Line Schedule Chart	

Users can choose from this rich array of functions to do their
programmerless Real-Time Report Processing creating real operational
control procedures. This is especially effective because the functions analyze
Report data producing a Result set of data which can then be further
refined by executing more functions including graphic or print processes.

Each user typically learns the analytic functions and options they use most. The primary functions of Search, Sort, Totalize and Match are very popular. These functions have equivalent functions that can do mass updates after the process is completed thereby providing great productivity in information update processing.

Iterative RUN utilities were provided to enable users to execute a function, save the completed function mask, alter the mask, and use it repetitively. The iterative RUN scripts created are:

IBINARY FIND   ICOUNT   IFIND   ISEARCH
ICALCULATE   IDATE   ISORT
ITOTALIZE

Two very powerful functions which have no equivalents in today's general purpose computer applications were provided at this time. One was the Count function and the other was the Calculate function.

The Count Function

The Count function is used to analyze and summarize data and statistics. Based on key fields, the Count function computes subtotals, percentages, averages, entry counts, and more.

The Calculate Function

The Calculate function is used to compute, compare, and replace numeric data, character strings, dates, and times in a Report. It has the ability to analyze Report data line by line and make logical decisions in the process.

The Calculate function is so functionally rich it is essentially an application development language in itself. One user was able to create a complete state and federal payroll process with this Calculate function alone. Another found it to be extremely valuable in the analysis and management of international monetary funds.

The MAPPER RUN script application development language also expanded in power and capability. All of the manual functions can be called with RUN script statements for execution in procedures. In addition to those functions, an extensive array of logic statements are also provided.

Additional RUN script Logic

Break Collected Data	If Conditional
Call Subroutine	Hide Window
Change Variable	Input Variable
Clear Abort Routine	Insert Variable
Clear Error Routine	Justify Variable
Clear Label Table	Language Select
Clear Link To Other RUNs	Last Line Number
Clear Subroutine	Link to Another RUN script
Close Window	Load Field Name
Command Handler	Load Format Character
Create Result Copy	Load System Message
Define Button	Load Variable
Define Constant	Load Variable Array
Define Edit Box	Local RUN Call
Define List Box	Network Off
Define Menu Box	Network Read
Define Text Box	Network Remote
Define Variable	Network Return
Define Window	Network RUNs
Exchange Variables	Network Sign-on
Execute Command	Network Write
Exit Subroutine	Out Variable To Display
Find and Read Line to Variable	Output Mask
	Peek Variables
Function Key	Poke Variables
Function Key Input	Pop Variables Stack
Go To Statement	Push Variables Stack
Hide Window	Read Continuous Data lines
Other System Read Data	Read Line
Other System RUNs	Read Line Next
Other System Sign-off	Read Password
Other System Sign-on	Refresh Screen
Other System Write Data	Register Abort Routine

Reg. Error Routine	Schedule RUN script
Aggregate Fetch	Statements
Aggregate Modify	Screen Control
Release Display	Server Interface
Remote RUN	Set Default Colors
Remove Variables	Set Format Characters
Rename Variables	Submit SQL Statement
Return Call Routine	Unlock Update Lock
Return Remote	Mass Update
Execute a RUN	Update Lock
RUN Status	Use Variable Name
RUN Subroutine	Wait Delay
	Write Line

Utilities were also provided to make RUN application design very efficient. RUN script statements can be generated from manual function execution with the Iterative utilities. Screen (menu) control logic can be generated with the SCGEN utility.

This makes it possible to present information in any way on the screen or in menus.

MAPPER systems are capable of supporting efficient, high volume real-time, random access, Real-Time Information Processing, along with large amounts of concurrent, real-time updating of the database.

These adjectives sound good but what do they really mean? What is considered efficient in a MAPPER system? How high is high volume? How real is real-time? What is the degree of randomness in access? What is the transaction mix in Real-Time Information Processing between manual functions and RUN executions? How much is real-time updating actually done in a significant MAPPER service? **To give these general terms some meaning statistics from a large-scale MAPPER service are detailed:**

It is estimated that this service provides annual savings of over $35 Million per year over alternate Reporting methods.

It gives strong testimony to the efficiency and potential of well promoted and Coordinated, user-designed, BIS/MAPPER Real-Time Information Processing system services.

The potential of MAPPER software functionality and RUN script design capability is to provide the most productive information processing and user application design environment in the computing industry.

The MAPPER RUN script language was so effective in rapid application development because RUN statements could call and execute the over 150 pre-programmed Real-Time Information Processing functions as part of their logic. Such analytic functions typically consisted of thousands of lines highly efficient assembler code which were pre-assembled. They automatically and efficiently perform major analytical processes such as search, sort, match, and calculate and resolve real-time database access and update conflicts.

Recovery, security and back-up procedures are also automatically provided and did not have to be programmed. Screen logic generators and dynamic debug tools accelerated development steps. The report structured MAPPER database also made database setup and design or modification easy and quick.

The macro analytic function logic, the logic generators and the automatic background support all have to be programmed uniquely for each application with other development languages. With these advantages, MAPPER software can be very efficient in application development compared to conventional programming methods.

The imagination and creativity of users as empowered with Real-Time Information Processing Information Power Tools and the RUN script language makes possible comprehensive, state-of-the-art application development by users or DP professionals.

RADS (Rapid Application Development Studio) system.

This is a toolset that magnifies the power of BIS by making it much faster and easier to create major business applications. It provides a structured development environment for use of BIS as a 4th Generation Language when designing comprehensive, major applications.

RADS is a complete Integrated Development Environment (IDE), with point-and-click wizards that eliminate the need for most low-level RUN script coding. As a result, BIS developers using RADS assemble, deliver and maintain major business solutions much more quickly and easily than ever before.

An early version of RADS was used to create PCME (Point & Click Environment), for selection of analytic function options which was integrated with BIS starting in 1999. The RADS toolset is itself a complex BIS application (written using BIS run script), a testimonial to the power and creative potential of BIS.

Chapter 8

MAPPER Systems Marketing Golden Age

By 1981, when MAPPER software products were authorized for world wide marketing, IS&C had these Mainframe MAPPER 1100 services in these Sperry plant locations:

Roseville MN. - (2) 1108 and (1) 1100/80 systems
Blue Bell PA Headquarters -   (1) 1108 system
Bristol TN -   (1) 1100/20 system
Salt Lake City UT -   (1) 1108 system
San Jose CA -   (1) 1100/40 system
Frankfurt Germany -   (1) 1108 system

A detailed description of these services is provided in this Chapter as well as successful marketing methods and the resulting customer base.

 MAPPER Real-Time Report Processing by its general nature is applicable in all industries, government and organizations.

By 1983, it was stated that 80% of new Sperry customers were buying because of MAPPER software.

At the peak of the success of MAPPER marketing shortly after the merger of Sperry with Burroughs to form Unisys, the MAPPER system market looked like this:

MAPPER 1100 Systems 1,500   USA
MAPPER 1100 Systems 1,000 International
MAPPER 1100 Systems 500   Japan
MAPPER 5 Systems   600
Personal (PC)Mapper Systems   6,500
UNIX MAPPER Mid Frame Systems 4,300

The MAPPER World

Registered Terminals	935,000
Registered Users	1,031,000
RUN script Designers	77,000
Active Reporting Applications	1,169,000
Reports On-Line	71,500,000
Stored Lines of Data	14 Billion
Lines Processed Per Day	61 Billion
Transactions Per Day	2.7 Billion

Representative MAPPER Customers At That Time:

Manufacturing
Unisys, General Telephone & Electronics,
McDonnell Douglas, Nike

Transportation
Santa Fe RR., Northwest Airlines, America West
Airlines

Distribution
Subaru of America, King Bearing, Kesko

Retailing
Circle K, Floral Network

Banking
Union Bank of Switzerland, TS Bank

Insurance
Employers Mutual,
National Life, Kansas City Life

Construction
Bechtel Corp., Sargent & Lundy

Energy Production
Northern States Power,
Kansas City Power & Light

Recreation
Walt Disney Enterprises, Carnival Cruise Lines

Government
Many Federal, State and City Governments
DOD, State of Minnesota, Westchester County
NY, Hillsborough County FL, California and
NYC welfare systems.

Military Branches
US Army, Navy, Air force
The Air Force had the most MAPPER Systems
+ Many more

To be used by Government and Military customers, sophisticated security capabilities had to be provided such as: Data Encription and dynamic Password changing. This was in addition to the user function, station and data access limitations normally Provided.

MAPPER Systems were translated for use in more than 15 foreign languages including Spanish, German, French even Chinese and Japanese.

At its peak under Sperry Corporation, MAPPER systems were installed world wide in a system base worth over $3 Billion.

Chapter 9

MAPPER Systems and Unisys Corporation

Burroughs and Sperry Corporations merged to form Unisys Corporation. MAPPER Systems, were renamed BIS, Business Information Server.

Considering the exceptional functional capabilities, ease-of-use, performance, networking, security, administrative controls, system auditing, recovery, history provision, etc., the MAPPER system is far superior to anything else – a giant step beyond any 4GL model of computer use. It supports the "1st Language" for user designed applications.

Since1968, Added functional releases has been made almost every year since then, hence its functional richness, which is unequaled in the industry. BIS is the World's most powerful productivity APP

User designed, Real-time Information Processing applications have enormous productivity potential and are applicable in the operation of all businesses and institutions from the smallest to the largest. Such productivity and upward compatibility across systems provide enormous tactical and competitive advantages for Unisys and its BIS customers.

No other IT vendors offer in one user executable, integrated, system scalable, high productivity real-time software system:

Functionality available across a wide range of industry systems
An equivalent user-driven set of >150 Information Power Tools with over 700 options
A Real-tme, User designed, Report Structured Database with interfaces to industry standard databases.

**A complete, powerful 1st Application Design
Language for Users**

**Extensive screen, edit and application code generation
Client-Server Networking across a range of system
sizes and vendors
Internet Integration and accessibility
A full set of system, user and database security
controls**

**Upward application compatibility from MS Windows
PC's to mid-frame and main-frame industry systems.**

**BIS systems software has been constantly upgraded
to run on all of these state-of-the-art systems:**

Unisys main frame OS 2200 ClearPath systems
Microsoft Windows Systems
LINUX Red Hat and SUSE Systems
SUN Solaris

**Interfaces are available to create application that
integrate the BIS system capabilities and database
with industry relational database systems such as:**

ORACLE, SYBASE, INFORMIX, MySQLServer
Object Database Connectivity (ODBC),
ADO.net; relational data access through Microsoft
NET Framework,
OLEDB; A Microsoft Object Linking and Embedding
Database
Messaging; Websphere MQ peer to peer Message
Queuing and Microsoft Messaging

**Unisys has continued to invest in OS 2200 BIS
Systems Development over the years and with
increasing emphasis on improved performance in all**

system versions as well as BIS systems modernization. These modernization concepts encompass:

+ A modern Graphic User Interface (GUI Point & Click)   look and feel for control of the interactive Information Power Tools
+ A modern application development environment.
+GUI, Unified system and database administration   utilities.
+ Tools to aid in modernization of existing applications.
+ Expanding interoperability with industry software environments.
+ Improved Internet operability and integration
+Development of a tablet computer interface to BIS systems.

BIS systems have been Web enabled with   the ICE Internet   Commerce Enabler. BIS-ICE is a software   integration   solution   that   allows organizations to manage dynamic Internet Web services on a corporate Intranet or the public Internet and World Wide Web.

Chapter 10

World Greatest Crypto APP:
Block-Chain + Real-Time
Information Processing

BIS Systems functional capabilities + its extremely fast database processing make BIS the ideal System for Block-Chain and Crypto information processing.

The BIS Report Structured (Spread Sheet Like) Data Base provides an excellent format for Crypto Exchange or Index data presentation

Its large,150 + instantly executable Information Processing Functions with 700+ Options such as: Search, Sort, Match, Calculate & Graphics
enable Crypto users to focus and refine Wallet, Ledger, Exchange and Index data to discover ideal profitability opportunities.

Crypto securities can also be enhanced with the ability to do User Registrations with

dynamic passwords, User specific Function and data access limitations,
The data base provides extremely efficient data updating with Encription and Decripton as needed.

Automatic Recovery and History development is provided with the system.

BIS Mapper, The World Greatest Crypto APP: Block-Chain + Real-Time Information Processing

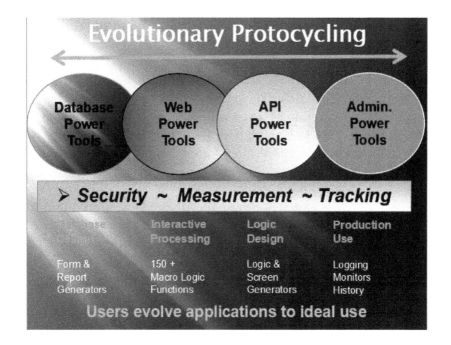

Applications can begin at any hardware level and evolve to meet all growth requirements with modern, "point & click" interfaces to over 150 interactive, Information Processing Power Tools (functions) with Over 700 options + real-time execution without programming, used on a shared, electronic filing cabinet report structured database, with full data base security, performance and application development and monitoring tools.

The universal potential for computer productivity with BIS Real-Time Information Processing is unlimited.

The fact that, originally, BIS/MAPPER systems required mid or main frame computing power for operation and can now operate on a laptop PC indicates how much conputing power is now available. Users, with their gifts of imagination and creativity, combined with BIS Real-Time Information Processing are users of the 1st Real-Time Application Design Language for Users. Application develop time is typically 1/3 the time using standard development languages and data base systems.

The BIS Report Structured (Spread Sheet Like) Data Base
provides an excellent format for Crypto Exchange or Index
data presentation

Its large,150 + instantly executable
Information Processing Functions with 700+ Options such as:
Search, Sort, Match, Calculate & Graphics enable Crypto
users to focus and refine Wallet, Ledger, Exchange and Index
data to discover ideal profitability opportunities.

Crypto securities can also be enhanced with the ability to do
User Registrations with dynamic passwords, User specific
Function and data access limitations,
The data base provides extremely efficient data updating with
Encription and Decripton as needed. Automatic Recovery,
Backup and History development is provided with the system.
Application development done in 1/3 the time of conventional
programming and data base systems.

Author Profile

Louis Schlueter is a data processing professional who is retired from Unisys after 34 years of service and experience in the industry. He held various technical, system test, engineering, manufacturing-planning as well as programming and management positions. He wrote the initial software design specification for Information Processing concepts on which the BIS/MAPPER system is based. He was also one of the initial programmers of the system.

He established the position and served as the MAPPER System Coordinator of the MSD MAPPER system in the Unisys Roseville, MN. plant. He was also instrumental in the development of the MAPPER system as a Unisys software product. He frequently consulted on the use of the system at Unisys user conferences, with Unisys marketing and at MAPPER system customer sites. He has written and had published numerous articles on MAPPER systems. He has also authored two books, "User-Designed Computing" and "User-Designed Computing, The Next Generation" in addition to this one.

BIS THE Killer Crypto App

Search for this book on Amazon
ISBN 13 978-1720989509
or Title ID: 8611692
at Createspace.com

For The Complete 262 page BIS/Mapper history and method of implementing User Designed Applications get the book:

Business Information Server, BIS THE Killer App

Search for this book on Amazon Books by Title, Author or:

TitleID: 8022133 at Create Space Publisher

ISBN-13: 978 1984004147
ISBN-10: 1984004147

For an Introductory MAPPER/BIS Video:
https://youtu.be/g3BsxG8EvOo